# THE WORLD OF
# FLORENCE NIGHTINGALE

## Kirsteen Nixon

# Important dates

| | |
|---|---|
| 1820 | 12 May: Florence Nightingale born in Florence, Italy. |
| 1837 | The Nightingales embark on a Grand Tour. Queen Victoria succeeds to the throne. |
| 1845 | Florence first hears of Kaiserswerth. |
| 1847 | She goes to Rome with the Bracebridges and meets Sidney Herbert. |
| 1849 | Elizabeth Blackwell becomes the first woman to receive a medical degree in the USA. |
| 1849–50 | Florence spends the winter in Egypt and spring in Athens, visiting Kaiserswerth on her way home. |
| 1851 | Second trip to Kaiserswerth. |
| 1852 | Florence studies hospital reports and designs, begins *Suggestions for Thought*. |
| 1853 | She takes a post at The Establishment for Gentlewomen during Illness and nurses cholera cases at the Middlesex Hospital. |
| 1854 | 28 March: France and Britain declare war on Russia; the Crimean War begins on 20 September: the Battle of Alma; reports of inadequate nursing. Florence and her nurses depart for Scutari Hospital, arriving on 4 November. |
| 1855 | Florence visits Balaclava and has her first attack of fever. |
| 1856 | The war ends and Florence returns home. |
| 1858 | She is elected as the first woman Fellow of the Statistical Society. |
| 1859 | Louis Pasteur suggests that micro-organisms may cause many human and animal diseases. |
| 1859–63 | Although very ill, Florence secures a Royal Commission for India, and publishes *Notes on Nursing* and *Notes on Hospitals*. |
| 1860 | The Nightingale Training School opens. |
| 1870 | Louis Pasteur and Robert Kock establish germ theory. |
| 1876 | 1 May: Queen Victoria is declared Empress of India. |
| 1901 | 22 January: Victoria dies and is succeeded by Edward VII. |
| 1907 | Florence is awarded the Order of Merit. |
| 1908 | She is awarded the Freedom of the City of London. |
| 1910 | 13 August: Florence Nightingale dies at her home in South Street, London. |

*Above:* Florence as a child, a pencil drawing by her sister Parthenope.

*Above:* Florence, Parthenope, Lady Verney, and Sir Harry Verney, at Claydon House, *c.* 1880.

# A remarkable life and legacy

Florence Nightingale is remembered as 'The Lady with the Lamp', who tenderly nursed soldiers during the Crimean War; but this was just one great period in a life of many celebrated achievements.

The story of her life reveals a complex and very private person, with a shrewd and analytical mind. Her dedication during the Crimean War gave her a worldwide reputation, but she only saw this as an opportunity for further work. She rejected convention to follow what she believed was her calling and devoted the rest of her life to reforming health care in the British army and the nation in general.

Against a backdrop of family disapproval and recurring ill health, she wrote over 200 books, pamphlets and articles, drove health reforms and sanitary improvements in Britain and India, and advised on and oversaw the development of the nursing profession.

Today her legacy can be found in nursing standards and hospital design principles, and she remains an inspiration to health care professionals around the world.

Her remarkable achievements have made her one of our greatest and most famous Victorians.

*Above: Miss Nightingale in the Hospital at Scutari*, engraving by J. Hind and G. Greatbach, 1856.

# A privileged childhood

*'For seven years of my life I thought of little else
but cultivating my intellect.'*

Florence was born in Italy on 12 May 1820, and was named after the city of her birth. She was the second daughter of wealthy English parents William and Frances Nightingale, who had been honeymooning abroad since their marriage in 1818. Their eldest child, Parthenope, also named after her birthplace, had been born a year earlier. The Nightingales owned two large country houses, Lea Hurst in Derbyshire and Embley Park in Hampshire.

Florence came from a remarkable, liberal family. Her maternal grandfather, William Smith, was a Member of Parliament for 46 years. He was a strong campaigner for humanitarian causes, the abolition of slavery and religious tolerance. He was also a supporter of the arts and artists.

Florence's father's surname was originally Shore. He inherited his fortune from his mother's uncle, Peter Nightingale, and with it changed his name. Uncle Peter, nicknamed 'Mad Peter', was considered an eccentric and was known as a wild gambler and heavy drinker. The inheritance, made from lead mining in Derbyshire, made William a wealthy country gentleman.

The two Nightingale girls spent much of their childhood in the country, spending the winters in Derbyshire and the summers in Hampshire. As they grew up it became clear that the two sisters were very different: Florence, a serious and solitary child who would often escape into her dream world, was devoted to her studies, whereas Parthenope was happier doing needlework and sketching. Many of Parthenope's drawings

*Below:* Lithograph from a drawing by Parthenope Nightingale of Embley Park, the Nightingales' home near Romsey, Hampshire, *c.* August 1856.

survive, and they provide personal pictures of their lives and surroundings.

At first the sisters were taught by a governess who followed their mother's instructions. Their days were spent practising French, going for long walks, reading the Bible, playing the piano, singing and drawing.

When Florence was 11 their academic education was taken over by their father who had been educated at Edinburgh and Cambridge. He held advanced views on the education of women and taught his daughters grammar and composition, mathematics, music, modern languages, Latin and Greek. This education was unusual for young ladies of the time, but Florence's thirst for knowledge meant that she could now pursue areas that interested her.

Her father gave her this remarkable education, but gave no thought as to what she would do with this learning. It did not occur to him that she would expect to be able to use her intellect and knowledge.

Despite this privileged setting Florence grew deeply unhappy. The triviality of her role as a young lady in fashionable society distressed her. She immersed herself deeply in her studies, seeking fulfilment there in what felt like an empty existence in a gilded cage.

*Above:* Pencil and wash drawing by Parthenope of Florence (on the left) reading and Marianne Nicholson, in the drawing room at Embley, *c.* 1830.

It is clear from Florence's early letters – which often included lists and tables of information, meticulously catalogued flower specimens, transcriptions of favourite poems, shell and coin collections – that she had a natural skill for classifying, analysing and documenting data. It was a skill she was to go on to develop and use in her future career.

*Above:* A poetry album owned by Florence Nightingale. The poetry was transcribed between 1832 and 1840, and the poets include Croly, Bloomfield, Wordsworth and Shelley. The album also includes the names of English flowers and extracts from books.

# The gilded cage

*'I hated the idea of being tied for ever
to a life of society.'*

In 1837 the Nightingales began a Grand Tour abroad. They were accustomed to foreign travel, and Florence was able to experience people's lives and cultures in other countries. Both at home and abroad she met important and influential people, some of whom would become her supporters and collaborators in the future. With every journey, she hoped to discover the answer to her calling.

The family travelled around Europe, where it was an exciting time, as revolution was in the air. Florence revelled in the good conversation and political intrigues, danced enthusiastically at balls and listened to music at La Scala, Milan. After meeting the exiled patriot Sismondi in Geneva, she became a passionate supporter of Italian freedom.

She dutifully made notes on scenery, art and architecture, and also on laws and social conditions. After her tour she admitted to herself that she had a desire to shine in society, but on her return to England her calling proved stronger.

Florence's religious beliefs were the driving force of her life and work. From a young age she had felt that she had a calling. On 7 February 1837, she had a revelation, a moment when she felt God called her to His service. It was a while before she decided that her calling was to be a nurse, but once she had, she was steadfast and determined.

*Above:* Perfume case designed to look like a book, containing five phials of perfume, padded by wool and in a hinged box. 'FN' is embossed on the lid and 'Quinte Essenza' on the spine.

*Left:* Pencil and wash drawing by Parthenope of the interior of a palace in Florence, 1838.

*Above:* Lithograph of a drawing of Florence by Hilary Bonham-Carter, her cousin, published in 1854.

Florence wrote about the lives of women of her class, which evolved into her novel *Cassandra*. In it, she explored the oppression of the educated and privileged women of Britain who, if allowed to use their intellect and talents, could contribute so much to life. Instead, they were confined to petty, boring duties within their families. Marriage was the only escape – but that brought its own confines and stifling life. Years later, suffragettes and feminists rediscovered this work, and found it an inspirational and valuable piece of writing.

Florence saw Parthenope as an example of the typical middle-class Victorian woman that she herself refused to become. Despite their differences they were both victims of the class and lifestyle in which they lived. They were both imprisoned in the same gilded cage.

In retrospect Florence realized that she had wanted to become a nurse from an early age. She accompanied her mother when visiting the poor and sick in the villages near their home in Derbyshire. Her concerns for the 'suffering of man' increased and so did the visits. Her family, and in particular Parthenope, complained bitterly about the time she spent in this.

As Florence's determination to have an independent life grew, so did her family's – and especially Parthenope's – opposition. Florence and Parthenope were brought up together and were only one year apart in age, but they were very different in temperament and aspirations. Florence was shy, neat and methodical while Parthenope was lively and artistic, but possessive and subject to tantrums. Parthenope disapproved of Florence's desire to be independent, but she was also jealous of her and the time away from family life that Florence's pursuits brought her.

*Above:* Florence Nightingale and her sister, Frances Parthenope, by William White (watercolour, c. 1836).

# Following her calling

*'You don't think that … I'm going to stay dangling about my mother's drawing room all my life. I shall go out to work, to be sure.'*

Once Florence had decided what she wanted to do with her life she set about planning ways to accomplish it. She had become friends with Dr Richard Fowler, physician of Salisbury Infirmary, and formed a plan to undertake three months' training there. When she announced this to her parents they were horrified. Her mother refused to allow it. 'Mama was terrified! The reason was not the physically revolting parts of a hospital, but things about the surgeons and nurses which you may guess …'.

In 1847, in the hope that it would distract her, Florence was sent abroad with Charles and Selina Bracebridge, a wealthy, childless couple. During this time, she met Sidney Herbert and his wife Liz, who both shared her interests: Liz accompanied Florence on visits to convents and hospitals while Sidney became an influential collaborator and friend. On the way home in 1850, Florence visited Kaiserswerth, a community in Germany consisting of a hospital, infant school, penitentiary, orphanage and training school for teachers.

*Above:* Pennant made by Florence from her petticoats, with her sister Parthenope's name (in Greek) in white tape. The pennant was tied to the mast of the dahibiyah (Nile boat) on which she travelled in 1849–50.

*Above:* Sarah Gamp, from Dickens' *Martin Chuzzlewit*: nurse, midwife and layer out of the dead.

In the mid 19th century hospitals were dirty and dangerous places, as the need for hygiene was not recognized. A sign of a good, experienced surgeon was if his apron was covered in blood. If you were wealthy enough you would be treated at home, and only those without hope would go into hospital. The character of Sarah Gamp, in Charles Dickens' *Martin Chuzzlewit*, was a popular image of nurses at the time. They were dirty and often drunk, and supplemented their income through theft and prostitution. A nurse's work was akin to being a servant or cleaner: it was not an occupation an educated young lady would even contemplate.

While in Athens in 1850, Florence saw some boys playing with a ball of fluff, which turned out to be a baby owl. She rescued the owlet, which she named Athena, and hand-reared her, carrying her around in her pocket. After Florence had left for the Crimea, the poor creature was neglected and died. Florence exclaimed, 'Poor little beastie, it was strange how much I loved you'. The bird was later stuffed.

*Left:* Athena, Florence's pet owl, when preserved.

*Above:* Pages from the lithograph book, *Athena*, produced by Parthenope, about Florence's visit to the Parthenon.

On her return the 30-year old Florence felt inspired by this experience of real nursing, yet she had no hope of any further training. Instead she gathered information about hospitals and health systems in England and abroad, working secretly in her room. She tried to behave like a dutiful daughter, but her private notes are full of misery and the pointlessness of her existence. At times, she wished herself dead.

Finally her family relented and agreed to allow her further training as a nurse so she returned to Kaiserswerth where she gained vital, practical experience. She made medicines, dressed wounds, witnessed amputations and was at the bedside of dying patients – all of which horrified her mother.

What impressed Florence most was the moral tone of Kaiserswerth. The nurses worked there because they cared about people's welfare: nursing was a vocation, not a means of making money. 'I find the deepest interest in everything here and am so well in mind and body. Now I know what it is to live and to love life.'

# Freedom at last

*'I am 30, the age at which Christ began his mission. Now, no more childish things, no more vain things, no more love, no more marriage.'*

Once Florence decided what her calling in life was to be, she set out to secure an independent life for herself. Marriage was out of the question. She had several marriage proposals but refused them all, including her cousin Henry Nicholson, a young suitor called Marmaduke Wyville and Sir Harry Verney, who later married Florence's sister, Parthenope.

The man she came closest to accepting was the philanthropist and poet Richard Monckton Milnes, whom she met in 1842. She knew it was a match her mother would approve of and she thought he would be sympathetic to her interests. However, she eventually turned him down. Afterwards, she seemed to have pangs of

*Above:* Richard Monckton Milnes, 1st Baron Houghton, one of Florence's suitors.

regret and for some time continued to consider the pros and cons of marriage to him. 'I have an intellectual nature which requires satisfaction and that I would find in him. I have a passionate nature which requires satisfaction and that I find in him. I have a moral and active nature that requires satisfaction and that I would find in his life ... I could be satisfied to spend a life with him combining our different powers in some great object. I could not satisfy this nature by spending a life in making society and arranging domestic things.'

When Florence came back from Kaiserwerth, her need for freedom persisted despite having to return to her family and domestic life. Those close to her realized that her depression and frustration would continue, and appealed to her mother to allow her to have some independence away from

*Above:* Lithograph of Florence with Athena the owl: a drawing by Parthenope, 1855.

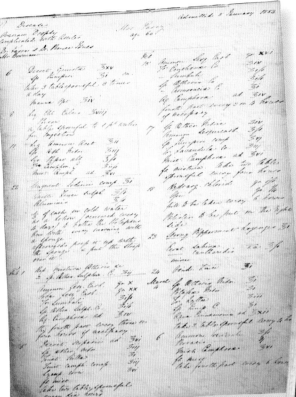

FLORENCE NIGHTINGALE
aged about 25     drawn by J.HBC

the family. Finally her mother relented and allowed Florence to go to Paris to train with the Sisters of Charity. Before she left there in January 1853, she was offered the position of Superintendent of The Establishment for Gentlewomen during Illness, London. Florence needed to secure a position so that she could start her working life. She accepted the post. Her father gave her an independent allowance of £500 a year: she had her freedom at last.

The Establishment was set up to care for well-educated, respectable gentlewomen – mostly governesses – who had a limited income and could not afford treatment. She was to select new premises, appoint a chaplain and manage the funds. At first the work suited Florence's nursing and administrative talents, and her management was praised by committee members, but she soon became restless.

After a year Florence decided to leave the Establishment and was considering taking a post at King's College Hospital, when a cholera epidemic swept across London; instead she took temporary leave to nurse the victims at the Middlesex Hospital. It was not long before Florence had another opportunity and another plan in mind.

*Above: Carte de visite,*1856.

# The nation goes to war

## *'I am now in the heyday of my power.'*

The British army entered the Crimean War on 28 March 1854. It was a war that saw the end of certain military practices – such as the sale of commissions – and the beginning of the use of new inventions, like the railway. It was the first time the public saw the realities of war.

At the outbreak of the war, British army procedures had remained unchanged since the Battle of Waterloo more than 40 years before. People at home were not aware of any problems until William Howard Russell, one of the first professional war correspondents, sent alarming reports to *The Times* about conditions at the front. The reports described the terrible plight of the soldiers: the poor supplies, the spread of disease and the lack of women nurses, compared with their French allies.

The Crimean War saw the first use of the electric telegraph in a war environment. This meant that Russell's reports could be sent home and published in the papers the next day. It was the first war to be photographed, most famously by Roger Fenton. Russell's despatches caused an outcry and pricked the conscience of the public about the hardships and suffering of the British soldier. The people demanded action.

Having seen the reports in *The Times*, Florence asked Liz Herbert for Sidney's opinion of her idea of taking a small expedition of nurses out to the Crimea. At this time Sidney Herbert was Secretary at War. In response to the public

*Above:* Bracelet made from the hair of Florence's father, mother, sister (Parthenope) and cousin (Shore), with a green enamelled heart-shaped pendant and snake's head clasp with pearls.

THE RUSSIAN HOSPITAL IN SEBASTOPOL.

*Left: The Russian Hospital in Sebastapol*, an engraving from *The Illustrated London News*, 6 October 1855, from a sketch by E.A.Goodall.

*Right: Soldiers in the Crimea, a photograph by Roger Fenton, c. 1855.*

*Below: Florence Nightingale and her nurses landing at Boulogne, en route for Scutari Hospital, an illustration on the lid of a box.*

Miss Nightingale & Staff Landing at Boulogne en route for the Hospital at Scutari.

outcry he asked Florence to lead a government-sponsored group of nurses to the military hospital in Scutari, Turkey. He pleaded, 'There is but one person in England that I know of who would be capable of organizing such a scheme ....'

Florence accepted the office of Superintendent of the Female Nursing Establishment in the English General Military Hospitals in Turkey. A committee, consisting of friends and her sister, started to recruit the nurses and applications came in from a variety of backgrounds. Florence insisted that the women should have nursing experience and practical knowledge of hospitals. Nursing sisterhoods were asked to provide nurses, although some refused because they would have to work under Florence rather than their Mother Superior. Only 38 suitable women could be found: 14 women with hospital experience, 14 Anglican sisters and 10 Roman Catholic nuns. Their terms of employment were quickly signed and the group set off for the Crimea on 23 October.

The party of nurses left London to travel overland to Marseilles where they joined the P&O packet boat *Vectis*, bound for Constantinople. The voyage became a nightmare when it hit terrible storms. One of the nurses in the party wrote, 'the top was blown off the cabin, the engineer's hand but washed off deck'. Florence was a poor sailor at the best of times and so suffered from bad sickness, keeping to her cabin for the entire journey. They arrived in Scutari on 4 November 1854, ten days after the Battle of Balaclava and the day before the Battle of Inkerman.

# Calamity unparalleled

*'Steeped to our necks in blood.'*

Upon arrival at Scutari, Florence and her nurses found the conditions at the hospital were far worse than the reports in *The Times* had suggested. They had been led to believe it was well-supplied, and they would have everything they needed, yet all kinds of essentials, including food and bedding, were lacking and the makeshift wards were filthy.

The wounded men had to suffer a long, rough boat journey to the hospital. Some, already suffering from cholera and malnutrition, died on the way or soon after arriving.

Florence greatly respected many of the army doctors and she paid close attention to army regulations. She insisted that neither she nor any of her nurses would enter a ward or attend a patient without the specific request of the medical officer in charge. Some of the doctors never accepted the nurses' presence and were, at first, reluctant to give them duties. Florence had a particularly uneasy relationship with Dr John Hall, Principal Medical Officer in the Crimea.

Determined that she would succeed in introducing female nurses into military hospitals, Florence set out to maintain rigid discipline amongst her staff. They were very restricted in what they were allowed to do: they were ordered not to talk to medical officers or to patients unnecessarily, and were not allowed in the wards after 8.30 p.m. Some of the nurses grew frustrated at these restrictions and the lack of opportunities to do real nursing. Some women, despite excellent intentions, were totally unsuitable for the environment and unprepared to accept the discipline and privations.

The duties of nurses at Scutari were similar to those of a domestic servant: washing, sewing and cooking. Only trusted and experienced nurses were allowed to dress wounds, but all nurses were faced with the grim realities of hideous injuries, frostbite and soldiers covered in fleas. Some of the nurses were totally unprepared for the hardships and complained about the conditions, the lack of food and their uniform.

A uniform was issued to distinguish the nurses from the other women in the hospital – the soldiers' wives and camp followers – and to ensure that they were treated with respect. It was ill-fitting, unflattering and uncomfortable. Accounts of what it looked like differ but it probably consisted of a dark grey wool jacket and

There was limited medical help for injured soldiers during the Crimean War, with only a few effective drugs available and the use of antiseptics not yet in practice. Many army surgeons were cautious of the use of chloroform: Dr John Hall warned against its use saying, 'The smart of the knife is a powerful stimulant, and it is much better to hear a man bawl lustily, than see him sink silently into his grave'. This may sound barbaric but it was based on an honest belief that if the patient was conscious and screaming then he would be more likely to survive.

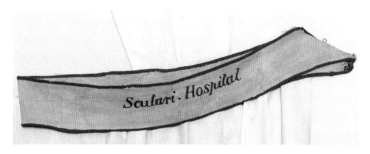

*Left:* Linen sash worn by nurses at Scutari Hospital during the Crimean War.

*Above: The Great Military Hospital at Scutari*, a coloured lithograph by Thomas Packer, 1855.

*Right: Scutari Hospital and Cemetery*, a lithograph from a drawing by William Simpson, 1856.

skirt, apron, cap and linen sash with 'Scutari Hospital' embroidered in red across it.

Rebecca Lawfield, who later became one of Florence's most valued nurses, complained bitterly about the cap she had to wear. 'I came out,

Ma'am, prepared to submit to everything ... but there are some things, Ma'am, one can't submit to ... and if I'd known, Ma'am, about the caps, great as was my desire to come out to nurse at Scutari, I wouldn't have come.'

# The general dealer

*'The strongest will be wanted to the wash tub.'*

At first, Florence did hands-on nursing, but she soon took charge of the administration of the hospital and the organization of the nurses. She observed the weaknesses of the management and haphazard distribution of supplies, and set about reorganizing them. She bombarded Sidney Herbert with requests for supplies and used her own resources to buy essential items, providing all sorts of things from socks and shirts to bedpans and operating tables. Florence also oversaw the distribution of the gifts that were sent by the public.

Florence introduced many measures to reorganize Scutari Hospital and to tackle the immense problems of hospital hygiene, but the death rate from disease continued to rise. What she was not aware of was that the hospital had been built over an open sewer, which had become blocked and was overflowing.

Back in Britain there was a change of government and Lord Palmerston became Prime Minister. He ordered a Sanitary Commission to go to the Crimea, to inspect and clean up the hospitals. They arrived at Scutari on 4 March 1855. As well as the clogged sewer, they found that the main water pipe into the hospital was obstructed by the carcass of a horse, and the toilets were blocked and leaking into the water-tanks. The sewers were flushed out, ventilation was added in the roof, the walls and floors were lime-washed, and orderlies were instructed to empty waste daily.

There was a dramatic drop in the death rate when the commission's work took effect, but this must have also been due to other factors. There were fewer casualties arriving at the hospital, which meant less overcrowding, and they were in better health when they arrived.

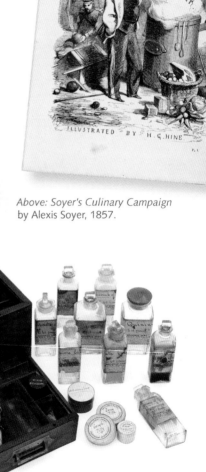

*Above: Soyer's Culinary Campaign by Alexis Soyer, 1857.*

*Above:* Florence's personal medicine chest, which she took to the Crimea.

During the Crimean War soldiers were given raw rations of food, which they were expected to cook themselves. The men often found that they did not have the means to cook it, the meat was generally bad and the rations were unsuitable for a sick person. Florence installed diet kitchens to provide appropriate meals for invalids. Alexis Soyer, who had been the chef at the Reform Club in London, volunteered to go out to the Crimea. He reorganized the kitchens and created new dishes from standard rations.

In May 1855, with Scutari Hospital in a more stable state, Florence decided to visit the other hospitals in the Crimea. A few days after her arrival in Balaclava, she collapsed from weakness and exhaustion, and was close to death. She had caught 'Crimean fever'. Once she had begun to recover a little she returned to Scutari and continued her convalescence there. She was able to begin to work again by September, but her illness was to have lasting consequences.

The weather, which had been bitterly cold, also improved. Florence fully supported the work of the commission and believed that it saved the army. The drop in the death rate at the hospital has been popularly attributed to Florence's actions, but she never claimed to be solely responsible and saw the improvements as being a team effort.

*Above: A Ward in the Hospital at Scutari*, a lithograph from a drawing by William Simpson, 1856.

# The birth of a legend

*'We could kiss her shadow as it fell and lay our heads
on the pillow again content.'*

For the first time the British public were aware of conditions under which the common soldiers had to survive during war and their consciences demanded that something should be done. There were soon reports and stories about a young lady who was tirelessly tending the soldiers.

Florence's work in Scutari went beyond cleanliness and basic nursing care: she restored humanity to the soldiers. She made arrangements for a screen to be put around a patient having an amputation, rather than have the operation in sight of another patient who may face the same fate tomorrow. She penned letters for the soldiers to their families and answered inquiries about missing or ill men. She wrote letters of condolence to the families of the men who died and sent money to their widows. This was perhaps the first war where an official person paid attention and care to the families of soldiers.

Testimonies from ordinary soldiers about their treatment in Scutari flooded home, praising Florence for her care and devotion. As she insisted that she was the only one allowed on the wards at night, she would patrol the four miles of beds, checking all was well. The first image of Florence as 'The Lady with the Lamp' was published in *The Illustrated London News* on 24 February 1855. It launched her to an iconic status, one which still remains today.

The legend of 'The Lady with the Lamp' gripped the world. Her fame impacted dramatically on her family and Parthenope became her manager at home, collecting cuttings about her sister, and circulating information and reports to family,

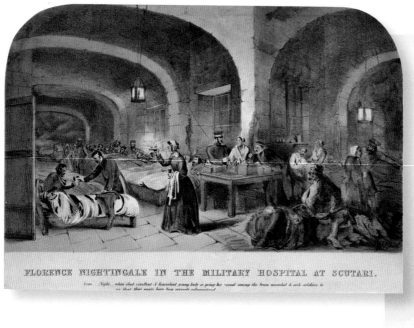

FLORENCE NIGHTINGALE IN THE MILITARY HOSPITAL AT SCUTARI.

*Above: Florence Nightingale in the
Military Hospital at Scutari*, a coloured
lithograph by J.A. Benwell, 1855.

*Right:* Turkish candle lantern
or lamp from Scutari Hospital,
used during the Crimean War.

MISS
NICHTINGALE

WE
WELCOME THEE BACK
to thy
NATIVE SHORE
MUSIC & WORDS
BY
E.C.CROGER.
RESPECTFULLY DEDICATED BY PERMISSION
TO
MISS NIGHTINGALE
ON WHOSE RETURN FROM THE EAST IT WILL BE SUNG
AT ALL PUBLIC AND PRIVATE REJOICINGS.

Accounts of Florence's constant care and attention were, by the nature of those who described them, sometimes misplaced. She was described as being at the side of all men at all times, but it must have been common for a sick soldier to presume that the tender lady by his bedside was Florence rather than another woman. Florence's fame unintentionally obscured the work and achievements of the other women during the Crimean War, and has continued to do so.

friends and acquaintances. Knowing that Florence would demand her privacy to be respected, Parthenope refused to consent to the release of photographs and pictures of her. Only two portraits, which had been drawn from life, were published with the family authorization, but they were expensive and not intended for the mass market. This meant that the demand for portraits of Florence became insatiable and had to be created from the imagination. Many depictions of her were romantic and idealized, and looked nothing like her. She appeared on inexpensive products like paper bags, and a series of affordable Staffordshire figurines was created in 1855.

Scores of songs and poems were written about her, but it was Henry Wadsworth Longfellow's poem *Santa Filomena* that secured the iconic image of 'The Lady with the Lamp'.

Florence saw the publicity surrounding her as vain, and felt it obscured the true disaster and suffering of the war. She only exploited her fame and image when it was needed to highlight her campaigns. Her desire for privacy and rejection of the limelight just seemed to attract people's attention more.

# Returning home

*'I am a bad mother to come home and leave you
in your Crimean graves.'*

Florence's unstinting devotion to duty brought about a transformation of Scutari Hospital, and earned her the admiration and respect of not only the soldiers she saved from disease and starvation, but of the entire nation. The war ended when the peace treaty was signed on 30 March 1856. Florence stayed at Scutari until the last of her nurses had left and her records were completed.

She left for England on 28 July 1856, travelling incognito under the name of Miss Smith. She made sure she escaped a hero's welcome by not letting anyone know her travel arrangements. On reaching London, she made her way to the Sisters of Mercy Convent in Bermondsey and spent the morning in prayer and meditation. She then took a train alone, heading to the little station of Whatstandwell in Derbyshire. Walking up the hill, she arrived at Lea Hurst unannounced on 7 August 1856.

Florence was thin and exhausted, still suffering with the symptoms of Crimean fever which would go on to plague her for the next 30 years. She shrank from the adulation she received on her return, and was in urgent need of rest and recuperation. Her mind was full of a sense of failure and burdened by the memory of the thousands of Crimean dead. 'I stand at the altar of the murdered men, and while I live I fight their cause ... nine thousand of my children are lying, from causes which might have been prevented, in their forgotten graves. But I can never forget ... it remains for us to strive that their sufferings may not have been endured in vain to endeavour so to learn from experience as to lessen such sufferings in the future by forethought and management.'

Current medical opinion of Florence's illness suggests that she was suffering from chronic brucellosis, originating in the Crimea. It was most likely caught from eating infected milk or cheese. Symptoms of brucellosis include fever, extreme physical and mental exhaustion, depression,

*Right:* Copeland Parian ware statuette of Florence Nightingale.

*Right:* Print inscribed 'Lea Hurst Sept/56. A troublesome sitter.' Florence arranged for William, a sailor boy, Robert, her errand boy, Peter Grillage, a little Russian prisoner, and Rousch, a Crimean puppy, to be brought back from the Crimea. She called them her 'spoils of war' and arranged for them to be looked after at the family home in Derbyshire.

*Below:* Florence Nightingale's dress, made from a wool/silk mix fabric, 1870.

loss of appetite, and severe pain and sciatica, all of which plagued her well into her 60s. For most of the rest of her life she suffered these bouts of ill health and on several occasions was close to death. During her illness she was confined to her room, often in bed. Viewed against this background of ill health, the work she was able to achieve over the next 20 years was truly remarkable.

The Crimean War was only a prelude: Florence's experiences in Scutari Hospital gave her knowledge and drive, and her fame gave her powerful influence. She was uniquely placed to instigate and lead reform. She was determined to fight the cause of the men she saw as having been 'murdered' and prevent a reoccurrence of the Crimea's high death rate. Devoting the rest of her life to the reform of army sanitary conditions at home and in India, and the planning of military and civil hospitals, she also laid the foundations of the modern nursing profession. This generated an enormous volume of letters, reports and publications of all kinds.

There are several theories offering alternative explanations for Florence's ill health, including lead poisoning from the mines near her family home in Derbyshire, chronic fatigue immune deficiency syndrome, post-traumatic stress disorder and stress-induced anxiety neurosis. There have also been investigations into her psychology to determine whether she suffered from bipolar disorder or was a hypochondriac.

# Her life's work

*'Nine thousand of my children are lying ... in their forgotten graves.*
*But I can never forget.'*

On her return from the war, Florence immediately set about ensuring that the mistakes that were made in the Crimean War were exposed and learned from. Within six weeks, she had enlisted Queen Victoria's support for a Royal Commission to investigate the health of the British army. The Minister of War requested that she write her observations and recommendations, based on her experiences, into a formal and confidential report. The ensuing report ran to 900 pages.

Florence lead all the stages of the Royal Commission's investigations, choosing

Florence was able to look at data, draw conclusions and create a picture in her mind of the results. She discovered that accurate statistics were the key to understanding how and why things happened. In 1860 she was elected first woman Fellow of the Statistical Society.

commissioners who became trusted and long-standing supporters and collaborators in her work. She worked with Dr William Farr, a pioneering statistician to create statistical diagrams to illustrate her findings in a clear and accessible way. Florence called these diagrams 'coxcombes' but to us they are the first pie charts. She found that more soldiers died from preventable diseases than from wounds, and that the mortality rate in Scutari hospital was higher than in any other hospital.

Florence's attention soon turned to the British army in India. She lobbied for a Royal Commission investigation, this time into the state of sanitation there, and was successful in 1859. Again she and her trusted collaborators began assembling data and facts. She discovered that no figures or records were kept and had to collect information at first hand. By 1862 the analysis was complete and her findings had became a 92-page report.

The full report was published in July 1863 and, being well aware that she needed public support for her projects, Florence was keen to publicize

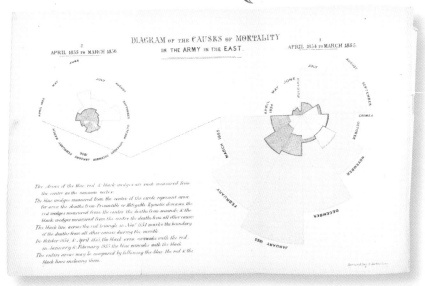

*Left: Notes on Matters Affecting the Health, Efficiency and Hospital Administration of the British Army* by Florence Nightingale, 1858.

the findings. She had advance copies sent to influential people and journalists, so that they could familiarize themselves with it before it went public.

The facts were appalling: soldiers were suffering with alcoholism, unsanitary barracks, poor water supply, primitive drainage and bad hospitals. By the end of her analysis she realized that reforming the health of the Indian army relied on reforming the health of the local population.

With a backdrop of recurring ill health, and almost without leaving her room, Florence became a leading authority on India. With her ability to analyse data and the unique statistics she had collected, she had the health of the whole country in her mind's eye. Following the publication of her findings, newly appointed viceroys and prominent officials came to see her before leaving for India and reported back to her.

The health of the British army in India and the civilian population there remained her constant concern for the rest of her working life.

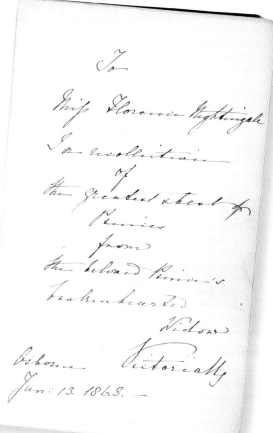

*Above:* Inscription by Queen Victoria to Florence Nightingale at the front of *Speeches and Addresses of the Prince Consort*, 13 January 1863.

*Left:* Florence Nightingale's report on the state of sanitation of the British army in India, 1863.

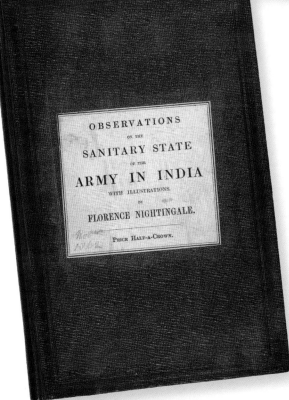

OBSERVATIONS
ON THE
SANITARY STATE
OF THE
ARMY IN INDIA
WITH ILLUSTRATIONS.
BY
FLORENCE NIGHTINGALE.

PRICE HALF-A-CROWN.

Florence meant her report to be provocative: she had been asked to write a convenient summary but instead took the opportunity to employ shock tactics. She presented a barrage of compelling statistics, again in collaboration with William Farr.

# The Nightingale Training School

*'Let us hail the successes of other training Schools, sprung up, thank God, so fast and well in latter years …'*

During the Crimean War contributions were sent by the public to Florence for her work. By the end of the 1850s more than £44,000 had been raised – more than £2 million in today's money. The money became the Nightingale Fund, intended to be used to establish an institution for the training, sustenance and protection of nurses and hospital attendants. It financed the Nightingale Training School for nurses at St Thomas' Hospital, London. Other training schools existed but these were all connected to religious orders which made the Nightingale School the first non-sectarian training establishment for nurses.

At the beginning of the school's life, Florence's attention was still concentrated on her work on India. She asked to be relieved of the responsibility of managing the school, although she was involved in its planning. She saw the value of working with an established hospital and chose St Thomas', partly because it was on the point of redevelopment and also because its matron, Mrs Wardroper, was committed to nursing reform. Mrs Wardroper became the first principal when the school opened on 24 June 1860.

An advertisement had been placed in *The Times* in May 1860 inviting applications to be the first probationers for one year's training. The probationer nurses were required to be 'sober, honest, truthful, trustworthy, punctual, quiet and orderly, clean and neat'.

During their training, probationers acquired fundamental nursing skills such as applying dressings and leeches, administering enemas, bandaging and ensuring a constant flow of fresh air into the wards. However, there was little formal teaching in the early years and probationers had to learn on the job with occasional lectures. In time, Florence became more actively involved and

appointed the first Home Sister and involved the St Thomas' surgeon, Mr John Croft, who established a much-needed system of lectures and examinations.

Florence began to meet probationers and sisters regularly at the hospital and wrote lengthy letters to her probationers which were usually read at the annual meeting or printed for private circulation.

*Left:* The Nightingale Training School badge.

*Below:* Mrs Sarah Elizabeth Wardroper, *c.* 1880, matron at St Thomas' Hospital from 1853 to 1887.

*Right:* Florence with her brother-in-law, Sir Harry Verney, and Miss Crossland, Home Sister of the Nightingale Training School, in the centre of a group of nurses at Claydon House, 1886.

*Below:* 'Nightingale' nurse Helena Riddick in uniform, c. 1896.

Speaight     178. Regent St. w.

Florence's greatest contribution was to popularize nursing as a respectable profession for women. Those who trained at the Nightingale Training School became matrons of hospitals all over the world, leading to the reform of nursing in hospitals, workhouses and the armed forces. Other nursing schools and a midwifery school at King's College Hospital were founded, and the first training scheme for district nurses was set up.

Florence's interest in the Nightingale Training School was quite intermittent but her association with it lent renown and esteem. Nurses taught there became known as 'Nightingales' and their training, with its rigour, discipline and attention to detail, gave them a strong sense of pride. Despite St Thomas' Hospital being partly destroyed in the Second World War, the school continued to thrive, only to be disrupted by the introduction in 1948 of the National Health Service. Changes in the way nurses were trained meant that the school could no longer stand alone as a training institution and it closed in 1996.

---

The influence of the Nightingale Training School spread in Britain and abroad through the migration of its nurses. Florence sent letters of warm encouragement and sometimes small gifts to these pioneers.

By 1887 more than 50 matrons had taken up posts; training schools were established in London, Liverpool, Edinburgh, Sydney and Philadelphia on the Nightingale model.

# Florence's notes

*'Nursing … is to put the patient in the best position*
*for nature to act on him.'*

Florence wrote *Notes on Nursing* as hints to teach people how to nurse at home. First published in January 1860, it was an immediate success, selling 15,000 copies in the first two months. The book explored her central beliefs for health and treating illness. She believed in nature's healing properties: fresh air, cleanliness, natural light, warmth and a good diet.

A thoughtful book, *Notes on Nursing* was written for the public. It blends everyday sanitary principles with observations based on her own experiences. Florence, with the major health and sanitary experts of the day, conformed to the popular theory that diseases were caused by miasmas (believed to be vapours from decaying matter). In 1867, Joseph Lister presented his theory that it was not miasmas that caused diseases and infections, but minute organisms – germs – in them, which needed to be killed.

*Notes on Nursing* was written before the acceptance of germ theory. The miasma hypothesis was soon proved to be wrong, but it had brought about many sanitary improvements. Measures to remove dirt and waste also removed germs. Florence did change her view and came to believe in germ theory, but continued to stress that prevention through cleanliness was better than cure.

The book was written over 150 years ago and yet contains ideas well ahead of their time: a holistic approach – looking after a person's mental and physical wellbeing, with sensitivity to patient needs – is key to recovery.

As a young woman, Florence had developed an interest in the function and planning of hospitals when frustrated at not being allowed to train as a nurse. She continued to collect and analyse plans of hospitals in Europe and the British Isles. She believed that nursing and medical care can only be performed properly in a well-designed hospital. In 1863 she brought all her ideas about hospital design into her report, *Notes on Hospitals*, which begins: 'It may seem a strange principle to enunciate as the very first requirement in a

NOTES ON NURSING:

WHAT IT IS, AND WHAT IT IS NOT.

BY

FLORENCE NIGHTINGALE.

LONDON:
HARRISON, 59, PALL MALL,
BOOKSELLER TO THE QUEEN.

Florence advocated the pavilion style of hospital, where the building has separate wings, connected by corridors. This means that patients were divided into spacious wards with windows positioned on opposite sides, allowing natural cross-ventilation. Drawing from her experience in the large open ward hospital at Scutari, the pavilion style also made the hospital easier to manage by making each pavilion a mini-infirmary.

*Left:* Florence Nightingale's *Notes on Nursing*, inscribed 'For Mrs Lowe Janry 1860 from Mrs F Robinson'.

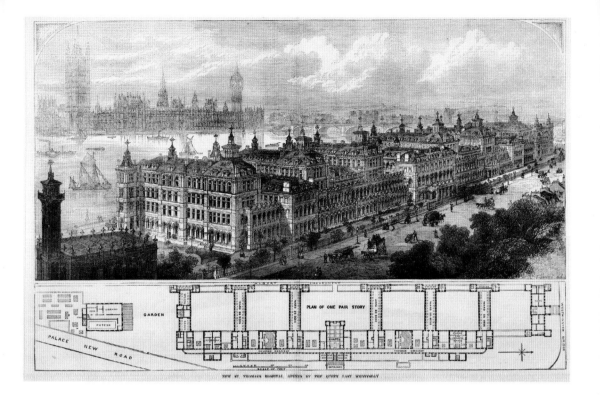

Hospital that it should do the sick no harm. It is quite necessary nevertheless to lay down such a principle.'

Requests for advice followed from hospitals in Britain and abroad, while the War Office asked her to advise on plans for new barracks and military hospitals. She was closely involved in plans to rebuild St Thomas' Hospital, advocating the use of pavilion wards (see panel), already in use at the Herbert Military Hospital at Woolwich, which opened in 1863.

Despite advising on hospital design and her continued work on improvements in them, Florence still believed that such places were dangerous and that the sick should be treated at home whenever possible.

*Above: New St Thomas's Hospital opened by the Queen last Wednesday*: an engraving from a drawing by J. Sulman, 1871, an elevated view of the hospital pavilions from the south-east with a ground plan.

*Right:* Florence Ward, St Thomas' Hospital, at the beginning of the 20th century.

# Two hundred publications

*'Sickness is not parochial, it is general and human
and should be borne by all.'*

Florence Nightingale is thought to have written over 14,000 letters and over 200 books, pamphlets and articles. She wrote on diverse subjects such as sociology, religion and philosophy, sanitation and army hygiene, hospital administration and statistics, Indian land reform, as well as her best-known works on nursing.

She contributed to and corrected government Blue Books on army reform, sanitary reform in India, and workhouse and Poor Law administration at home. She also wrote prefaces and introductions to other people's works supporting the causes she believed in. Some of her publications are not widely known, rare because she published them privately and only distributed them amongst friends or influential people whom she targeted or thought might be interested.

As well as the Nightingale Training School, the Nightingale Fund money was used to establish a midwifery school at King's College Hospital, London. At first the school was successful but after only six years it was closed after an outbreak of puerperal fever (a fever contracted during

*Above:* An unfinished oil portrait of Florence, 1868.

*Right:* Photograph album inscribed, 'To Miss Florence Lees, given by the Sisters, Nurses and Probationers of St Thomas's Hospital in affectionate remembrance of the time which she spent as a Nightingale Probationer amongst them. Easter Day 1864.'

*Far right: Notes on Nursing,* inscribed by Florence Nightingale to Florence Lees, 1877.

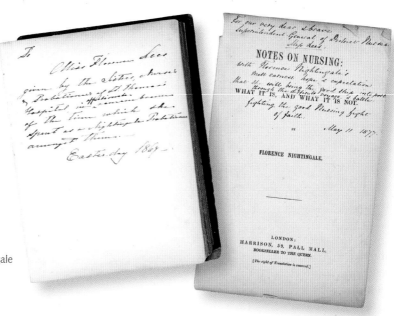

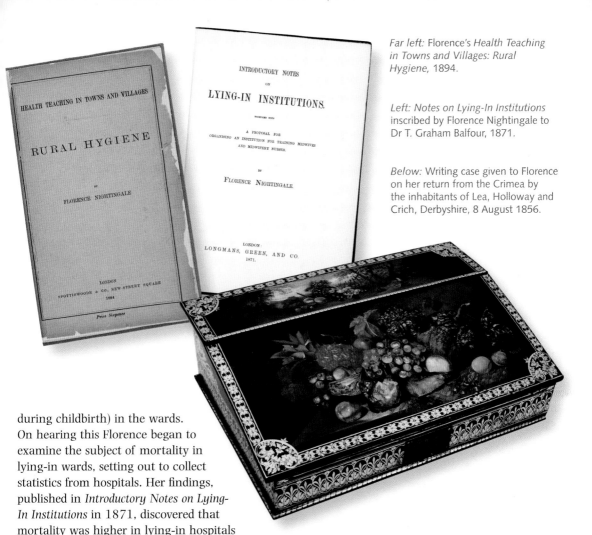

*Far left:* Florence's *Health Teaching in Towns and Villages: Rural Hygiene*, 1894.

*Left: Notes on Lying-In Institutions* inscribed by Florence Nightingale to Dr T. Graham Balfour, 1871.

*Below:* Writing case given to Florence on her return from the Crimea by the inhabitants of Lea, Holloway and Crich, Derbyshire, 8 August 1856.

during childbirth) in the wards. On hearing this Florence began to examine the subject of mortality in lying-in wards, setting out to collect statistics from hospitals. Her findings, published in *Introductory Notes on Lying-In Institutions* in 1871, discovered that mortality was higher in lying-in hospitals than at home. She concluded that it was safer to deliver a baby at home, however poor and unhygienic the conditions, due to the risk of cross-infection in hospitals.

In collaboration with Liverpool philanthropist William Rathbone, Florence played a vital part in the introduction of district nurses. She gave intellectual leadership and supported a network of pioneering nurses taught at the Nightingale Training School. Again, this campaign was conducted in writing and mostly from her sickroom.

The introduction of district nurses in Liverpool was successful and by 1886 the Metropolitan District Nursing Association had been established in London. Miss Florence Lees, a graduate of the Nightingale Training School, was appointed first Superintendent-General.

Florence wrote one of her last publications on nursing at the age of 74. In *Rural Hygiene* she continued to voice her concern for the health of everyone, including the poorer in society. Florence had overseen many revolutionary reforms in the areas of hygiene and sanitation, yet even in her advancing years she was able to devise and articulate new ideas, and look forward to the future.

Florence was passionate about the need to introduce trained nurses into workhouses: it was another area that she pursued into the last decade of her working life. The principle of professional, free health care being available to all can be seen as one of her more lasting achievements, and was only fully achieved with the foundation of the National Health Service in Britain in 1948.

**29**

# The final years

*'My friends drop off one by one, and I hang on …'*

During her lifetime, Florence continued to be remembered as the angelic 'Lady with the Lamp'. This was perpetuated by her desire to work in private and her ill health which kept her confined to home. She worked around the times when she was incapacitated, and conducted interviews with politicians, medical experts and Indian officials in her room. Time spent with her family and friends took second place.

In 1865 she moved to 10 South Street, a small house near Park Lane, London, and lived there for the rest of her life. She outlived many of her trusted friends, colleagues and family, but her network of advisors and collaborators grew as she added newer and younger experts, and as cabinet members and MPs came into office. Although she worked in private she did not work in isolation: she always sought advice and opinions from experts on her data and drafts.

Florence's sister Parthenope had married Sir Harry Verney in 1858. His family home, Claydon House, near Aylesbury in Buckinghamshire, became a second home for Florence. She often made arrangements for important visitors from abroad to be entertained in this historic country mansion. She also put Sir Harry to good use: as a Member of Parliament for Buckinghamshire, he introduced Florence's work to the House of Commons, so much so that he was nicknamed 'The Member for Miss Nightingale'. After Parthenope's death in 1890, Florence made longer visits to Claydon House, where she had her own apartments. She was fond of the young Verneys, especially as she lost so many relatives and friends.

Florence continued to write into her 80s, until her eyesight and memory began to fail. Until towards the end of her life she was still called upon for advice, but action was left to others.

She received testimonials and honours from across the world. In 1907 King Edward VII awarded Florence the Order of Merit, a great honour presented to individuals for particular achievement in the fields of the arts, learning, literature and science: she was the first woman to receive this. The following year she became the first woman to be awarded the Honorary Freedom of the City of London.

Florence died in her sleep on 13 August 1910, aged 90, at home in South Street. Her family

*Above:* Portrait in oils of Right Honourable Sir Harry Verney Bt (1801–94).

*Left:* St Thomas' Hospital sisters and nurses arriving at St Paul's Cathedral for Florence Nightingale's memorial service, 20 August 1910.

*Right:* Florence at South Street, London, 1906.

*Right:* Postcard entitled 'Miss Florence Nightingale's grave showing the many floral tributes', August 1910.

declined the offer of a burial at Westminster Abbey and she was, as she had wished, buried at St Margaret's Church, East Wellow, Hampshire.

Florence's ideas completely changed society's approach to nursing and her legacy remains strong today. Her holistic approach was well ahead of its time. Her work and fame inspired people – such as the founder of the Red Cross movement, Henry Dunant – and lots of men and women became nurses and put her ideas into practice.

During her lifetime 'Florence' became a popular name for girls, and also for all sorts of new inventions and designs, street and building names.

Today her achievements are still commemorated, with many hospitals and hospital wards named after her. Her birthday is an important date in the calendar for nurses, who attend a service at Westminster Abbey to honour her life and work. The service celebrates the professions of nursing and midwifery, and all

staff – both qualified and unqualified – working in these services are invited to attend. Florence championed causes that are just as important today, from hospital hygiene and management to the nursing of soldiers during war and afterwards, and health care for everyone around the world.

Florence Nightingale has continued to be remembered, on postage stamps and even a £10 note. The centenary of her death in 2010 was marked by many activities, celebrations and commemorations, including a set of stamps and a special issue £2 coin.

*Right:* This special issue £2 coin, first minted in 2010, marks the centenary of Florence Nightingale's death.

# Places to visit

Below is a list of places of interest with links to Florence Nightingale that are well worth a visit. Further information and details of opening are available on their websites.

**Florence Nightingale Museum, St Thomas' Hospital, London**: the story of the life and legacy of Florence Nightingale. 020 7620 0374; www.florence-nightingale.co.uk

**St Thomas' Hospital Central Hall**: a statue of Florence Nightingale. 020 7188 7188; www.guysandstthomas.nhs.uk

**Crimean Monument at Waterloo Place**: a statue of Florence Nightingale.

**St Paul's Cathedral**: a memorial dedicated to Florence Nightingale is in the crypt. 020 7246 8350; www.stpauls.co.uk

**Westminster Abbey**: a chapel named after Florence Nightingale. 020 7222 5152; www.westminster-abbey.org

**South Street, Mayfair, near Hyde Park**: a blue plaque where Florence's home used to stand.

**Claydon House, Buckinghamshire**: the family home of her sister and brother-in-law (National Trust). 01296 730252; www.claydonestate.co.uk

**St Margaret's Church, East Wellow, Hampshire**: Florence's burial place. 01794 323562; www.wellow-nightingale.co.uk

**Florence Nightingale Museum at the Selimiye Barracks** (Scutari) is still an army barracks and is open by appointment only. www.florence-nightingale.co.uk/cms/index.php/crimean-war/scutari-barracks

Information correct at time of going to press.

*Above:* The memorial to Florence Nightingale in St Paul's Cathedral crypt.

*Left:* Florence's room with its four-poster bed at Claydon House.